3-D
Baby Animals

■SCHOLASTIC

D0095717

Early Days

Some animals need lots of help when they are born. They need to be fed, cleaned, and protected by one or both of their parents until they can take care of themselves. Other animals have to fend for themselves from the moment they are born.

▼ Hold tight!

A mother squirrel monkey carries her tiny baby on her back until it's two months old. Once her baby reaches ten months old, it's almost completely independent of its mother.

A scorpion carries her young on her back until the bodies of the baby scorpions have toughened up!

▶ Fluffy chick

A duckling is born with a layer of soft, fluffy feathers to keep it warm. Within hours of hatching from its egg, a duckling can walk, swim, and even find food.

▲ Get up, stand up

Baby horses, or foals, can stand up and run just two hours after birth. To survive, herd animals, such as horses, must be able to run away and escape from danger at an early age.

Puppies and

D ogs and cats play a big part in many people's everyday lives. Dogs can perform a variety of tasks including protecting people and property, farm work, and helping people with disabilities. Cats are easy to care for and make excellent companions. At first, they were used to keep mice away from people's homes. Now they are the world's most popular pet.

▲ Furry friends

Dogs and cats don't always get along, but if you introduce them at a young age, puppies and kittens can live together.

If a mother cat thinks her kittens are in danger, she picks up each one by the skin at the back of its neck and carries it to safety!

Kittens

▼ Playing ball

Kittens love to chase moving objects. They can entertain themselves for hours by play-fighting. In the wild, this kind of behavior is important, as it teaches kittens many of the skills they will need as adults, such as how to follow and capture their prey.

▲ Puppy love

All puppies are born blind and deaf. They stay close to their mother until they're about seven weeks old. Puppies need her milk and warmth, and she also keeps them clean! Once they're eight weeks old, puppies are more independent and are ready to go to a new home.

On the Farm

Chickens, pigs, cows, and sheep are farm animals. These animals are raised for their meat, milk, eggs, and warm wool to make clothes. One of a farmer's jobs is to care for them when they're born and keep them healthy.

A hen turns her eggs as often as five times an hour and clucks to her unborn chicks, who will even chirp back!

▼ Smelly piglet

Piglets have an excellent sense of smell and love to sniff out bits of food that are buried under the ground. A piglet has a long snout with a flat nose and large nostrils.

◀ Baby milk

Baby cows, or calves, feed on their mother's milk until they are eight or nine weeks old. Dairy cows can produce up to 25 gallons (95 liters) of milk per day—that's 400 glasses of milk!

▼ Bleat! Bleat!

Lambs are usually born in the spring, when the weather is warmer. A lamb stays with its mother until it is about five months old. It recognizes its mother by her bleat, which is the sound she makes.

Monkeys and

Monkeys have long arms and legs for leaping and swinging through the trees. They feed on leaves, fruit, flowers, eggs, and even small animals. Apes are related to monkeys and are similar except that they have no tail and are often bigger and more intelligent.

▲ Strong bonds

Male orangutan babies stay with their mothers for the first seven or eight years. But a female orangutan stays with her mother until she is in her teens. She watches how her mother cares for her young, which in turn helps her to become a better parent.

Apes

▶ Big family

Macaque monkeys are very social animals and live in big groups called troops. When a baby macaque monkey is born, its older sisters help to take care of it as well as its mother.

▼ Slow walkers

Gorilla babies are born helpless. They don't learn to crawl until they're around two months old, and they only start to walk by the time they are five to six months old.

The pygmy marmoset is the world's smallest monkey and does not grow more than 5–6 inches (15 cm) long!

Let's look at
Emperor

These tiny monkeys come from South America. The babies are nearly always born with a twin, like the two below, but sometimes there are emperor tamarin triplets!

CUTE-O-METER

BABY FILE

Name: Emperor tamarin
Home: Brazil and Peru
Eats: Fruit, nectar, flowers, eggs, snails, spiders
Size: Tiny! Even as adults they will weigh less than a pound (454 g)!

Lara and Lucy's story

Little Lara and Lucy were born at the Denver Zoo and were orphaned when they were only three weeks old! Luckily, their older brother, Paddy, was around to help take care of his baby sisters.

Tamarins

A regal look

Emperor tamarins are named after Emperor Wilhelm II of Germany because the white facial fur they grow as adults looks a lot like his mustache did!

Hold on tight

Baby tamarins have strong hands and feet that they use to cling to trees, their parents, or the people who sometimes care for them.

Bear Babies

Baby bears are called cubs. A bear cub stays close to its mother until it's around two or three years old. A mother bear teaches her cubs all of the skills they will need to survive in the wild, such as where to find the right food, catch prey, and avoid danger.

At birth, bear cubs weigh less than a pound (454 g). They can't see or hear, and they have no fur or teeth.

◄ Bear claws

A bear cub's strong front paws and sharp claws are ideal for climbing trees. One of the first things a mother bear teaches her cubs is to climb trees to search for food and hide from danger.

► Water fight!

Play-fighting is important for bear cubs, as it teaches them to protect themselves and helps them grow stronger. Bears are very good swimmers and often swim in lakes and rivers to cool off, play, and chase prey.

▼ Motherly love

A mother polar bear usually gives birth to one or two bear cubs inside an icy den. Polar bear cubs learn to stay very still while their mother hunts. If they move, their mother disciplines them by swatting them with her paw!

Giant

Giant pandas belong to the same family as bears and have thick, shaggy coats. In the wild, they live only in the cold mountain areas of China.

Panda babies

A mother usually gives birth to two cubs, but often only one will survive. For the first few months, baby pandas can't open their eyes, and they hardly move until they are three months old.

Like mother

A baby panda learns by copying its mother's behavior, including walking, climbing trees, and eating bamboo. It depends on its mother for food and feeds on her milk until it's nearly a year old.

Pandas

Branching out

Once it's around two years old, a panda begins to take care of itself. It spends most of its time in the trees eating bamboo. Giant pandas eat 20–45 pounds (9–20 kilos) of bamboo shoots each day!

CUTE-O-METER

BABY FILE

Name: Giant panda
Home: China
Eats: Mostly bamboo
Size: A newborn baby panda weighs only 3–5 ounces (85–142 g), but an adult weighs up to 250 pounds (113 kilos)!

Wild Dogs

African hunting dogs, wolves, and foxes are known as wild dogs. But even pet dogs belong to the same family as wild dogs. All dogs have very strong teeth and jaws, but their eyesight is weak, so they rely on their excellent hearing and powerful sense of smell to hunt and catch prey.

◄ Baby fox

Early in the spring, fox cubs are born in a den, called an earth. Once they're about three or four weeks old, they begin to explore their surroundings. Their mother is usually not far away and keeps a close eye on her cubs. Adult foxes live alone or in pairs, but they live in family groups while their young cubs are growing up.

▶ Dog-sitting

African hunting dogs live in packs on the grasslands of Africa. Pack members help to raise the young pups. While their mothers are out hunting, other members of the pack watch over the pups and protect them.

▼ Littermates

Brothers and sisters born at the same time are called littermates. Wolf pups grow quickly, and by the time they're eight months old they have already become skilled hunters.

A wolf's sense of smell is so powerful, it can smell things that are up to 2 miles (3 km) away!

Big Cat Cubs

The big cat family includes tigers, leopards, lions, and cheetahs. Cats are carnivores, which means they eat meat. They are expert hunters with powerful bodies and sharp teeth and claws. Newborn cats cannot see or hear for several days, so they're protected by their mother until they can survive on their own.

▶ Small beginnings

At birth, a tiger cub weighs only 2 or 3 pounds (1 kg). But adult tigers can be up to 11 feet (3 meters) long from nose to tail and weigh up to 670 pounds (300 kilos)!

Tiger cubs begin to eat meat that their mother has caught for them when they're around two months old.

▲ Hunting lessons!

A mother cheetah looks after her cubs for more than a year, teaching them all the skills they'll need to survive. Sometimes, she will even catch prey and bring it back while it's still alive so her cubs can practice hunting for themselves.

◀ Who's the daddy?

Lions live in family groups called prides. Each pride has one male, several female lions, called lionesses, and their young, called cubs. The male lion protects the pride from predators, such as hyenas and other male lions.

Let's look at

African

BABY FILE

Name: African elephant
Home: Africa
Eats: Grass, leaves, fruit
Size: An elephant calf weighs between 176 and 264 pounds (80–120 kilos) and is the world's largest newborn baby land animal.

Center of attention

A new calf gets a lot of attention from all the adult elephants. It's protected and cared for not just by its mother, but by all of the female elephants in the herd.

African elephants are the world's biggest land animals. They live in groups, or herds, on the grasslands and in the forests of Africa.

Elephants

Trunk lessons

Just like a human baby, an elephant calf needs a lot of practice to eat and drink. It needs to learn how to use its trunk to bring food and water up to its mouth.

Mother's milk

As soon as it's born, a mother elephant helps her baby calf get to its feet. It has to be able to stand up and drink her milk in order to survive.

r--ssl--m--

Grasslands are large and mostly flat areas of land with very few trees. Many of the animals here are plant-eaters, such as rhinos, giraffes, and antelopes. But predators, such as lions, also live here, so many grassland animals stay safe by sticking together in large groups, or herds.

◀ Hornless

A baby rhino's horn doesn't grow until it's older. With no horn to defend itself, its mother carefully protects her baby from predators, such as hungry lions, that share its grassland home.

At birth, a rhino weighs around 70 to 90 pounds (30–40 kilos) and only ten minutes after it's born it can already stand up!

Babies

▼ Wobbly legs

One hour after it's born, a baby giraffe can stand on its long, wobbly legs. At first, it stays near its mother for protection because it can't run very fast.

▼ Keep quiet!

A mother antelope hides her baby, or calf, in a secret spot. She returns every few hours to feed it. The calf must stay very still so it doesn't attract attention from hungry predators.

Water Babie

These baby animals are champion swimmers and spend most of their lives either in or near the water. Their bodies are perfectly formed to suit their watery worlds. Some live near icy water, so their skin is extra thick to keep them warm. Others have smooth bodies or large flippers that work like paddles in water.

▲ Ice pups

A baby harp seal is born on the ice. Its mother recognizes her pup from all the others by its particular smell. After two weeks, the pup is left to fend for itself, even though it can't swim or find food until it's four weeks old. At this time, a pup is in danger of being attacked by hungry polar bears.

▶ Milk on the move

Dolphins spend their whole lives in water, even though they must come to the surface to breathe. A baby dolphin can drink its mother's milk while it's swimming!

▼ Water baby

Hippos are so big and bulky that they are happiest when floating around in the water, where they can keep cool. A baby hippo is born in shallow water and can walk and swim just minutes after being born.

A hippo's teeth grow continuously throughout its life and can reach up to 20 inches (50 cm) in length!

Emperor

Daddy care

A mother penguin lays her egg and then leaves it behind! She heads back to sea to feed, leaving the father penguin in charge. He carefully rests the egg on his feet and protects it until the penguin chick hatches.

Emperor penguins are the only animals that stay on the ice during the freezing Antarctic winter. During these freezing cold months, penguin chicks are born and raised.

Penguins

Chick-sitting duty

After several weeks, the mother penguin returns and takes over the babysitting. She keeps her baby chick warm by keeping it close to her body.

BABY FILE

Name: Emperor penguin
Home: Antarctica
Eats: Mostly fish and squid
Size: At birth, a baby emperor penguin chick weighs just 4 to 6 ounces (120–160 g).

Penguin pals

Once the penguin chicks are older, they huddle together in a group, called a crèche, to keep warm. Their parents go back and forth to sea, returning with food for their chicks.

Scaly Babies

These scaly babies belong to a group of animals called reptiles. They include crocodiles, turtles, snakes, and lizards. Most reptiles have dry, scaly skin and hatch from eggs. Baby reptiles look like tiny versions of their parents and can usually take care of themselves as soon as they're born.

▶ Good mom!

A mother crocodile lays around fifty eggs in a mound of rotting leaves near the water's edge. As soon as she hears the tiny grunts of her babies, she uncovers the eggs and helps the baby crocodiles open their shells. When they're born, baby crocodiles are just 8 inches (20 cm) long.

► Race to sea!

Tiny sea turtles hatch on a beach and have to rush to the water before being eaten by hungry seabirds and crabs. Only a few survive, but those that do can grow to be up to 5 feet (1.5 meters) long!

The Galápagos tortoise is not only the world's largest tortoise, but it can also live to be over 100 years old!

▼ Dragon babies

Horned lizards look like tiny dragons and are found in desert areas in the western U.S. and Mexico. Baby horned lizards are born with a full set of sharp, spiky horns on their heads and along their backs!

You might think you know all there is to know about baby animals, but here are some more facts about amazing babies.

Thumbs up!

At birth, a baby kangaroo is no bigger than your thumb! It has to wriggle up through its mother's fur until it reaches the safety of her pouch. The baby, or joey, lives in there until it's big enough to survive.

Armed to the teeth!

It's hard to believe that this cute little cub will grow up to be one of Africa's scariest predators—a hyena. Unlike many baby animals, hyenas are born with their eyes open and a full set of teeth!

Hunger call!

A baby owl grows a layer of soft, downy feathers to keep it warm. It needs to eat a lot of food, like mice, so it calls loudly to its parents whenever it gets hungry!

A baby koala spends its first six months inside its mother's pouch and the next six riding on her back!

This edition
created in 2013 by
Arcturus Publishing Limited
26/27 Bickels Yard, 151–153
Bermondsey Street,
London SE1 3HA

ISBN 978-0-545-62110-6

12 11 10 9 8 7 6 5 4 3 2 1   14 15 16 17 18 19 0

Supplier 01, Date 0913, Print run 2864

Printed in Rawang, Malaysia 106

First Scholastic edition, January 2014

Author: Samantha Hilton   **Editor:** Becca Clunes   **Design:** Top Floor Design Ltd
Picture credits: Shutterstock   **3-D images:** Pinsharp 3D Graphics